POCKET
INSPIRATIONS ON
ETIQUETTE IN
BUSINESS

POCKET
INSPIRATIONS ON
ETIQUETTE IN
BUSINESS

STUART NELSON

To order additional copies of this book, contact:
Xlibris
1-800-455-039
www.Xlibris.com.au
Orders@Xlibris.com.au
808100

Stuart Russell Nelson

Meet the Coach

Don't judge yourself by the past; you don't live there anymore. Life in front of you is far more important than that one you left behind.

At the age of twelve, I wasn't leaving a summer camp. I was leaving an orphanage, an environment with surroundings and events which produced psychological terror and humiliation. I was now moving back into a world I had forgotten, with a severe stammer and consumed with shyness.

Huge self-belief and mentors whose teachings didn't hold back helped me write my story by pushing me into becoming an effective leader, to be driven by my talent and my instincts and, more importantly, to own both my decisions and as to who I am, without apologies.

In later years, with my life's story still a work in progress, I was still managing my anxiety. That being so, I had now moved up from employee to CEO in both the advertising industry and the commercial film industry, during which time my expertise came from my worldwide coalface experiences, to include line producing television commercials in Australia, New Zealand, Hong Kong, and the USA, winning international awards including gold, and achieving the pinnacle award in amateur acting.

An experienced executive waiter in corporate boardrooms and private homes, I am now principal and published author at the Business Etiquette Consultancy.

In life, we all have choices and challengers. We walk faster, talk faster, eat faster, and communicate faster. This fast-paced reality is amplified in most businesses. I wake up each day wanting to inspire people and help them with their Etiquette in Business skills knowledge, which will add their value to the workplace.

These learnings may sound a bit ho-hum, but listen up: understanding protocol and manners in business is not a luxury item; it is a necessity.

Not everything may seem relevant today or tomorrow, but one day, they will be of extreme value to you.

If you can expand your knowledge on what were once possibilities to what will now be within the boundaries of your thinking, your outcomes will be amazing. You will discover best practices, which will explode you with self-confidence; encouraging face-to-face relationships; opening communication, allowing for appreciation of the choices you make in an atmosphere of friendship, imagination, and laughter.

From the fourteen topics that I cover, here are 150 fundamental skills of what are needed to add value to both yourself and your workplace. You will grow through them. You will learn through them. You will ensure that your employer will receive a return on their investment in you through them.

Maybe you have already started up that corporate ladder; then use this as a refresher course.

Let's get started. Your journey starts now.

CONTENTS

YOUR HANDSHAKE
SETS THE TONE

THE WHITEBOARD

Main handshakes that communicate differently:

The Upper Hand
The Double Hander
The Left-Hand-Side Advantage
The Elbow Grasp
The Pausing
The Pumper
The Lingerer
The Disabled Handshake

YOUR HANDSHAKE SETS THE TONE

Everything from your appearance to your introduction sends signals to colleagues, clients, and friends about you and your fit in the company. Your handshake should set the tone; it is presented in many different forms. Each delivers a different message.

YOUR HANDSHAKE SETS THE TONE

Handshaking is a classic example of non-verbal communication. It will set the tone for your introduction, to distinguish you from the pack. It is much more than saying *hello*; it is saying *this is who I am*.

YOUR HANDSHAKE SETS THE TONE

Handshaking is common but not universal;
be aware of cultural differences.
There is something powerful about a
person who gives you an appropriate
eye contact when handshaking.

YOUR HANDSHAKE SETS THE TONE

A proper handshake engages the others person's full hand, meaning the web between your thumb and index finger should be touching your partner's, with hands flat enough so your palms are touching.

YOUR HANDSHAKE SETS THE TONE

Do you remember a handshake that has stuck in
your mind? Who shook first? Who let go first?
Was the person nervous or relaxed?
Did they say their names or just 'Hi'?
Did they look at you or the next person?
What did you learn from it?

THE JOB INTERVIEW

THE WHITEBOARD

- ✓ Research both the employer's website and your own social media posts.
- ✓ Don't walk in with your iPad or mobile in your hand.
- ✓ Your mirror is your true friend; know your facial expressions.
- ✓ Punctuality is vital; be ten minutes early. Smile to everyone, including the receptionist. The interview process may start at the reception desk.
- ✓ Don't keep watch gazing.
- ✓ Use the interview to learn. Focus on what skills you will gain.
- ✓ Avoid just saying *yes* or *no*.
- ✓ Send a handwritten thank-you note a day after to the interview, reinstating your strong interest in the job.
- ✓ Being unfamiliar with your own résumé will ruin a great interview.

THE JOB INTERVIEW

The interview is the most important first step
in your working life *before* you get a job.
There is no magic formula, given that a great
number of the jobs are never advertised.

THE JOB INTERVIEW

The reason the job exists is because there is
a gap in their business. To be successful, you
must be able to demonstrate that you can
solve their problem better, quicker, faster.
The hiring manager will be listening very closely to
hear how credible your answers are. If you tell the
truth, you don't need to have a good memory.

THE JOB INTERVIEW

If you are really struggling and you have a
mobile phone, film yourself in a mock interview
situation with a family member or friend. It
may be difficult watching yourself on film,
but it allows you to spot your mistakes.

THE JOB INTERVIEW

Never walk into an interview cold.
Practice your answers to anticipated questions,
practice your handshake, practice your *hello*
and *goodbye*, practice sitting and standing, and
lastly, practice your prepared closing statement.
You must have a will to prepare.

THE JOB INTERVIEW

Most skills can be learned, but it is difficult to train people on their personality. The first thing the employer looks for is somebody with a personality that fits within the company's culture. Your personality is the key.

THE JOB INTERVIEW

There is a unique you.
You shine best being your natural self. Are you
suited to a large corporate firm or a smaller,
more entrepreneurial organization? Employers
are looking for those who will work within
the team. Dress for the job you want.
Take time to discover yourself.

THE JOB INTERVIEW

The hiring manager could make up their mind
about you within a couple of minutes. How they
can decide so fast? You've barely spoken a word.
Surprise, surprise! Hiring managers are just
human beings and sometimes make fast
judgements that they may regret later.
Know the company by their mission
statement and discuss what you will do
to add your value to their company.

THE JOB INTERVIEW

Lots of smart questions will be asked.
Specific responses are less important than other
factors like the quality of your conversation; you just
might be being tested for something else entirely.

THE JOB INTERVIEW

There will always be someone who has
a more impressive résumé or who does
interviews like a pro. These you can't control,
but there are things you can control.
Job seekers who are better polished,
personable, and well-mannered tend to
cultivate a better interpersonal relationship.
Learn from this.

THE JOB INTERVIEW

Have the ambition to want to constantly
commit to being the best version of yourself.
Play to your strengths; don't waste time and energy
in explaining things you probably don't do very well.
Know well what you do. Do well what you know.

THE JOB INTERVIEW

'Sorry, the job went to a competitor.'
But you gained from the experience. Learn
from the setback and diversion, analyse your
performance; it will make you stronger and wiser.
There is always another interview.

YOUR INTRODUCTION
TO THE WORLD

THE WHITEBOARD

Learning another person's name is the first,
most basic step in showing respect.

- ✓ Focus on the person.
- ✓ Repeat his or her name aloud.
- ✓ Repeat his or her name silently.
- ✓ Make a vivid association.
- ✓ Conclude the interaction with his or her name.

We all want to hear our own names spoken by
others.

HELLO

The mastering of introductions is an art, putting
you and the people you are introducing at
ease. The highest-ranking person is introduced
to everyone else in order of their position;
in simple terms, the first name mentioned
belongs to the most important person,
even if the client is eighteen years old.
'Liz Ainsworth, I would like you to meet
Hanna Jones, our new receptionist.'
'Hanna, Ms Liz Ainsworth is our managing director.'

HELLO

You are meeting someone for the first
time; it should be exciting. Where have
they been? Where are they going? In
life, how might they influence you?
Will you influence them?
Use both your names when introducing yourself.

HELLO

What's in a name? Everything!
Pay attention as to how people introduce
themselves; they are telling you how
they would like to be addressed: Sir,
Lady, Professor, Doctor, or Captain.
Use their title; they have earned that right.

HELLO

Always stand for an introduction; by remaining
seated, you could be perceived as having a
'you have just interrupted me' attitude.
If you are meeting a person who is disabled,
a handshake may not be appropriate;
wait until a hand is extended to you.

HELLO

Have you ever watched people doing the
introduction handshake ritual? Usually the one
party initiating that handshake is either looking
at the ground when saying *hello* or looking to the
next person waiting to be introduced to. Most very
rarely make eye contact. Doing this, they are seen
as persons lacking in confidence and personality.
Have you done that?

HELLO

Have you never used a false name when introducing yourself? *No!* Bet you have. You are talking in a small circle of people; after a few minutes, you will say, *'Hello, I'm Jack Bytheway.'* Why do you need to change your last name?

HELLO

Regardless of your career status,
branding yourself makes you visible.

- ✓ Why do you buy a certain car? The brand.
- ✓ Why do you buy certain clothes? The brand.
- ✓ Why will people buy what you have to offer? Your brand.

The excitement is not the buying
of a branded product;

- ✓ it's in the execution of
- ✓ Driving that car,
- ✓ Wearing those clothes, or
- ✓ Implementing your new knowledge.

ADD YOUR VALUE TO
THE WORKPLACE

THE WHITEBOARD

Executive presence isn't just fluff.

✓ It's your body language.
✓ It's your communication skills.
✓ It's your confidence.
✓ It's your social skills.
✓ It's how you should dress for a client meeting.
✓ It's your polished personal style.
✓ Do you show authority?
✓ Do you show trustworthiness?
✓ Are you competent?
✓ Are you likeable?

There is no clear definition. It is something that you will know when you see it. If you've got a minimum of, say, 80 per cent of the above, congratulations, you have a strong executive presence.

ADD YOUR VALUE TO THE WORKPLACE

Your business journey will have many destinations. Where you want to stop off is your decision; what part in it you want to play is your decision. Do you want to be a foot soldier or a leader in your field of expertise? That's your biggest decision. What game do you want to play?

ADD YOUR VALUE TO THE WORKPLACE

You will learn from reading a textbook, but you
will be empowered from life's experiences.
Business Etiquette knowledge creates
harmony, respect, and growth within
and outside the company.
You will find them awesome.

ADD YOUR VALUE TO THE WORKPLACE

I once had a severe stammer; having a flaw in your DNA, no matter what your social anxiety, does not affect your intelligence or your ability to achieve. Be patient with yourself; it takes a while to see things through a different lens. Your hidden talents could be what separate you from the pack. Show the world what's inside you.

ADD YOUR VALUE TO THE WORKPLACE

Limitations are just signposts.
They may signal different routes or different ways to
reach a destination, but they won't prevent you from
getting there unless you empower them to do so.
Ignore them, focus on your journey.

ADD YOUR VALUE TO THE WORKPLACE

Start each day with self-belief.
If colleagues believe in you, that's your cue to start believing in yourself. Don't read from the same road map as others do, and please don't walk like the slowest person. Work smarter, not harder. Love your job and perfect your performance.

ADD YOUR VALUE TO THE WORKPLACE

With your self-belief, you don't need a
reason to be more confident; just make
a decision to be more confident.
You don't need people to tell you that you
are amazing, that you are beautiful.
You don't need to leap over tall buildings. You
just need to wake up one day and say out loud,
'Today I am going to show self-belief.'

ADD YOUR VALUE TO THE WORKPLACE

How do you explain it when some people
succeed and others fall short?
Is it because they are smarter or
because they are lucky?
In my experience, it is *neither*.
Find your self-belief; it *will* lead you to
success. Here a word of caution: Success
is setting goals that feel true to who you
are, not to what others expect of you.

ADD YOUR VALUE TO THE WORKPLACE

Ensure that your manager understands your skill set, the efforts you put in, and the end results you produce. A bit of boasting is not bad, and it will help you at your review time. Keep a paper file if you receive complimentary emails.

ADD YOUR VALUE TO THE WORKPLACE

In life, you will overlook opportunities; we all do. Be an optimist; optimists go forward. Take advantage of opportunities. Open doors and step in; the doors that you open each day will decide which pathways you travel.

ADD YOUR VALUE TO THE WORKPLACE

We all have choices and challengers.
We are all made differently. We all view
things differently. You don't have to
be totally different to be unique,
just one or two core strengths.

ADD YOUR VALUE TO THE WORKPLACE

There is very little difference in people, but
that little difference makes a big difference.
Different people will give you different
perspectives, challenging you to
have a point of difference.
It is not about your race, religion, gender, or
education; it is all about your willingness to succeed.
Only you have a final say as to what
person you want to become.

ADD YOUR VALUE TO THE WORKPLACE

You must have a point of difference.
You are your brand. In this increasingly competitive
environment, your brand needs to have a number
of unique attributes creating this little difference.
What is your point of difference?
Think about your workplace: are you different
from your workmates, the way you dress,
communicate, your work attitude?

ADD YOUR VALUE TO THE WORKPLACE

Your desire for success should be far greater than fear of failure. Have self-belief. Be more informed. Be more polished. Be more embracing of change. You will then add more stamps to your passport.

ADD YOUR VALUE TO THE WORKPLACE

It's a common saying, *people
judge a book by its cover.*
Should you judge people by the way
they look or by their actions? It's not how
you look; it's how you think and act.
My having a speech hesitation—
I didn't come from outer space, but that didn't
stop me from becoming fodder for ignorant
people. That's what it is: ignorance, judging others
without having insight knowledge of them is
simply ignorance. You don't get points for that.

ADD YOUR VALUE TO THE WORKPLACE

If you have anxiety, create an alter ego, basing it on someone you admire and respect. Dare to be different. Your alter ego will give you the freedom to be a bigger, bolder version of yourself, enabling you to work within the team's spirit, maybe emerge as a team leader.

ADD YOUR VALUE TO THE WORKPLACE

Why do we create an alter ego?
Pursuant to the secrets act,
Bruce Wayne was Batman; Clark
Kent was Superman.
You may be presenting in front of a group of
clients, workmates, or superiors; it can be seriously
intimidating if you're normally timid and shy.
It shall be lawful for you to assume a cocky,
confident alter ego when it is time for you to
do a presentation in front of your peers.

ADD YOUR VALUE TO THE WORKPLACE

Whatever you do, stay in character!
Your alter ego will seem more real and authentic
if you commit to your performance. If you flip-
flop between your new identity and your old one,
people will see you as a person in a costume.

ADD YOUR VALUE TO THE WORKPLACE

It's really, really important to surround yourself with a team whose opinions you trust, who are not frightened to disagree with you. You have to listen. You are nothing without a good team.

ADD YOUR VALUE TO THE WORKPLACE

If you start to question what people are doing to the left of you, to the right of you, you will lose that clarity of thought. Listen to the information, process it; in the end, the decision has to come from who you are.

KNOW BASIC BODY LANGUAGE

THE WHITEBOARD

- ✓ Eyes up to the right—you're reaching for information from your memory.
- ✓ Eyes up to the left—there is a good chance your answer is being invented.
- ✓ Someone who makes hand gestures while speaking is generally a good communicator.
- ✓ Two fingers from one hand pressed against lips indicate holding back information.
- ✓ If your listener is constantly nodding and smiling, you are probably in trouble.
- ✓ If you ask, *'Do you understand?'* and they reply, *'I'm pretty sure that I do'*, you can assume that they don't.
- ✓ A formed fist covered by the other hand shows a feeling of aggression and frustration even when smiling.
- ✓ Talking with your hands out and palms upturned is a 'trust me' sign. Someone who isn't telling the truth is likely to conceal their hands.
- ✓ Drumming fingers shows restlessness and impatience.
- ✓ Leaning forward displays interest.
- ✓ Hands on hips show aggression, being authoritative.
- ✓ People who keep fingers closed and their hands below their chin when they talk command the most attention.

KNOW BASIC BODY LANGUAGE

Some people are inherently more social than others.
Properly used body language can be your
key to greater success on any level, to work
easily in a multicultural world, to influence
people and give you effective communication
skills to increase personal confidence.

KNOW BASIC BODY LANGUAGE

Body language is your silent command.
How do fortune-tellers produce an accuracy
of about 80 per cent when *reading* a person
that they have never met? It's not *magical*;
it is simply a process based on the careful
observation of body language, verbal signals,
and an understanding of human nature.

KNOW BASIC BODY LANGUAGE

Where a person places their cup immediately after
they take a drink is a strong indicator as to whether
or not they are open to what you are saying.
I have found that if they are feeling negative
about what they are hearing, they will place
their cup to the opposite side of their
body, forming a single-arm barrier.

KNOW BASIC BODY LANGUAGE

You can't fake body language because the
body tells the truth when the mouth is lying.
It reveals not what you are saying but what
you are both thinking and feeling.

KNOW BASIC BODY LANGUAGE

The world we live in is a multicultural society. With
your multicultural friends, do you understand their
body language? What are they trying to convey?
Unintentional miscommunication is possible.
Keep the mind open and acceptable
even if what you see and experience does
not make sense for you sometimes.

KNOW BASIC BODY LANGUAGE

Mirroring body language is a non-verbal way to say
'I am like you.'
However, I discovered that if you want to intimidate
those who are trying to prove their superiority to
you, mirroring their body language will disarm them.

KNOW BASIC BODY LANGUAGE

Can you distinguish a real smile from a fake smile?
A fake smile pulls back the mouth; a real smile pulls
back both the mouth and eyes. The more you smile,
the more positive reactions others will give you.

DRESSING FOR MOST OCCASIONS

THE WHITEBOARD

Clothing colours can influence your thinking.

✓ Dark colours are perceived as more normal, dominant, and authoritative.
✓ Light colours make the wearer appear more friendly and approachable.
✓ Some bright colours convey confidence and energy.
✓ Muted colours are conservative and less threatening.
✓ Contrasting colours can also send a certain message.

The higher degree of contrast, such as that of a black suit and white shirt or a navy suit and white shirt, can create a very powerful image.

DRESSING FOR MOST OCCASIONS

Some clothing choices will enhance your
reputation or detract from your credibility.
Don't judge others and dismiss being judged.

DRESSING FOR MOST OCCASIONS

Has there been a time when you have dressed to
gain attention, to impress, to play out your fantasy?
It starts with us as children right through
to our growing up years where hopefully
we have more dressing control.
Dress for your personality, and your work culture.
Don't dress for others.

DRESSING FOR MOST OCCASIONS

Have you invested in a home full-length mirror
so you can see yourself from all angles?
I bet you don't know what you
look like from the back.
I have found that most of us have a
'what we don't see' attitude.
Walk down a street and observe
people from their back.

DRESSING FOR MOST OCCASIONS

You may have exceptional skills, your unique
talent may make you special; however,
workplace dress code still applies to you.
Don't limit yourself.

OFFICE CONDUCT
AND BEHAVIOUR

THE WHITEBOARD

Eight responses never say to your boss:

✓ **That's not my job.** It's a negative, anti-team attitude.

✓ **Yeah, no problem.** You know you can't or won't complete the project.

✓ **It's not my fault.** Maybe it isn't. Instead of placing the blame, focus on offering to fixing the problem.

✓ **To be honest with you.** When this phrase is used, something negative is going to follow.

✓ **I don't have enough time for that.** Your boss is giving you much more to do because you are trusted; work with them.

✓ **I don't know.** This is a resistance to find the answer. Be proactive; say, 'Let me look into this.'

✓ **I can't.** Successful leaders have a can-do spirit. When you say 'I can't' to your bosses, they will hear 'I won't.'

✓ **I have always done it that way.** Every company has a different culture, a different way in reaching the same goal. Acknowledge and respect it.

OFFICE CONDUCT AND BEHAVIOUR

The world is constantly changing.
Have you ever felt that embracing change is
one of the hardest things you can do? You have
three choices. You can lead. You can follow.
You can resist change and remain stagnant.
Rather than fearing it, denying it, or
hiding from it, *embrace* change.

OFFICE CONDUCT AND BEHAVIOUR

Never underestimate your potential.
Chart your own course. Consider a career move
forward every eighteen months to two years. This
could be either a promotion, new responsibilities,
or a change of scenery.
Discover to live life on your terms.

OFFICE CONDUCT AND BEHAVIOUR

Realise that leadership is about accepting change.
It will refocus you; it will renew your interest and
opportunities, which in itself will be world-changing.

OFFICE CONDUCT AND BEHAVIOUR

Understanding that we live in a multicultural society, the sets of rules for good social skills are based on values that work for our culture and for people from their countries, from meeting socially to doing business to dining—skills that must be learned, remembered, applied, and constantly enforced.

OFFICE CONDUCT AND BEHAVIOUR

Average success is based on setting average goals.
Decide what you really want to be:
the best, the most admired, the most
challenged. Aim for the ultimate.

OFFICE CONDUCT AND BEHAVIOUR

Different offices have different policies
on office behaviour. There's no limit as
to how far opportunities can take you
if you embrace the office culture.

OFFICE CONDUCT AND BEHAVIOUR

Office politics and gossip result from
fear, boredom, or lack of purpose.
It hurts and there's a good chance it may not even
be true, but mud does stick. Instead of gossiping
about people, successful people talk about ideas.

OFFICE CONDUCT AND BEHAVIOUR

In life, maybe you didn't have a great start.
Bad things happen but bad things pass,
so now is the time to start being great.
Your yesterdays were just training days;
learn from yours and others' mistakes.

OFFICE CONDUCT AND BEHAVIOUR

'Show me your friends and I'll show you your future.'
The people and influences you surround
yourself with play a huge role in how you
think, act, and form your aspirations.
Everyone you meet should be your mirror.

OFFICE CONDUCT AND BEHAVIOUR

Company-sponsored social events—
these are rife with opportunities
to torpedo your career.
Anything that starts with the word *company* means
a business event: *company* Friday night drinks,
company BBQ, *company* social club function.
In all cases, workplace rules apply.
Oh, slipping unopened alcohol
into your bag is stealing.

OFFICE CONDUCT AND BEHAVIOUR

There are a few universal truths that you
need to be aware of at all times.
No matter how busy and dedicated you are
towards your work, you are probably going to not
score any points if your conduct isn't acceptable.

OFFICE CONDUCT AND BEHAVIOUR

Conflict in the workplace is any situation that leads to a disagreement between two or more individuals. The disagreement usually flows from misunderstanding about expectations and needs.

OFFICE CONDUCT AND BEHAVIOUR

Surprise, surprise!
The bathroom cubicle is neither a library
nor a telephone booth. Don't use them for
reading office memos or magazines and
making mobile phone conversations.

OFFICE CONDUCT AND BEHAVIOUR

Texting is hearing only your half of the conversation.
Wouldn't it be more friendly, personable,
and enjoyable to simply telephone them?

OFFICE CONDUCT AND BEHAVIOUR

It's a small gesture but a strangely refreshing one.
Delete that tired, outdated message on your
voicemail. Replace it with a new, upbeat version.
Present a positive change.

OFFICE CONDUCT AND BEHAVIOUR

There's a saying, *you never get a second chance to make a good first impression.* Nowhere is this truer than in the workplace. Using good manners is fundamental to a healthy workplace. With your job, you must learn what not to do, but at the same time, you must have fun at work.

OFFICE CONDUCT AND BEHAVIOUR

Some office breakout rooms cannot cope
with all staff eating at the same time. If you're
going to eat lunch at your desk, keep it
simple; you don't share your lunch, so why
share your home-made-lunch smells?

BOARDROOM HOSTING
IS A SKILL

THE WHITEBOARD

Instructions for your waiter:

✓ Your names and titles
✓ The guests' arrival and departure times
✓ The timing of the pre-meal drinks
✓ Will the special guest speak before, during, or after the main meal?
✓ When will the special guest eat, if at all?
✓ Is there a guest(s) with dietary requirement(s)?
✓ Where is their seating position(s)?
✓ The serving times for all meals
✓ The departure time.

BOARDROOM HOSTING IS A SKILL

Corporate dining hosting is a skill, probably the most powerful game in town. Entertaining in all industries is a given. When hosting other captains of industry, you must display confidence, leadership, and awareness, while being charming and attentive.

BOARDROOM HOSTING IS A SKILL

Ensure that your reception has a complete list of your guests, their title and company. This will ensure that on arrival, the receptionist will give the guest a warm company welcome.

BOARDROOM HOSTING IS A SKILL

Update your guest research.
You need to give yourself some ammunition that you can fire at them so they can boast about themselves. Show interest when they're bragging about their recent overseas trip or a recent promotion which changes their company status.

BOARDROOM HOSTING IS A SKILL

Seating guests at your home
dinner party can be fun.
In your boardroom, it's deadly serious. It
needs a good mix of *your people* with *their
people* to help conversation flow, maximising
the benefits for both companies.
It's your host's privilege for the
seating arrangement; don't change
the order to suit yourself.

BOARDROOM HOSTING IS A SKILL

If your guests are followers of the Muslim religion or any number of other religions, an awareness and acknowledgement of dietary and other cultural customs will prevent embarrassment. Even offering alcohol may give offence.

BOARDROOM HOSTING IS A SKILL

Briefing your waiter should be high on your agenda. The waiter is a temporary member of your staff; the link between the kitchen and the dining room, an important asset in keeping the food service on schedule.

BOARDROOM HOSTING IS A SKILL

As host, you must take total control of the
conversations from the *hellos* to the *goodbyes*.
The *clinking of the glass* to gain attention should
not be in your bag of business social skills.

BOARDROOM HOSTING IS A SKILL

Whose rule is Chatham House Rule?
The Chatham House Rule on confidentiality should
be firmly in your repertoire. This is an expression
used in most boardrooms or function rooms,
uttered by the chairperson or the host where
confidential discussions are taking place. It is
used worldwide to facilitate both free speech and
confidentiality at meetings. Meetings may be held
on the record or under the *Chatham House Rule.*

BOARDROOM HOSTING IS A SKILL

Are you a caring host?
Usually the guests won't begin eating if the host is talking. A hot meal is meant to be eaten hot. Think about when your guests are sitting around the table with their delivered hot food getting cold. Being a caring host is how you gain respect. Invite your guests to eat when they receive their hot meal.

BOARDROOM HOSTING IS A SKILL

Tea/coffee, maybe chocolates have
been served. The meal is drawing to a
conclusion. Guests are diary controlled.
As the host, you must be conscious of this.

RESTAURANT HOSTING
SECRETS

THE WHITEBOARD

Your Restaurant Hosting Checklist

- Don't just show up. Nothing is more awkward or unprofessional than taking a guest to a restaurant and being forced to wait for a table.
- It may seem like a minor thing, but if your plans change, please cancel your reservation; it can save a restaurant a lot of money.
- Are there going to be non-eaters in your party? Some restaurants have policies that all seated guests partake in a meal.
- Make sure the restaurant knows of any dietary restrictions your party has at the time your reservation is made.
- Shh, who's that at the next table?
- Don't be a table paper spreader.
- Don't take mobile photos in the restaurant.
- Make notes in pencil.
- Don't leave your mobile on the table; your guests are your priority. It should be out of sight unless you are expecting an important call that is pertinent to your lunch meeting, in which case, alert your guests
- Seek out and thank your waiter before leaving.

RESTAURANT HOSTING SECRETS

The quality of the selected restaurant
will reflect back on your company.
In selecting a new restaurant, while you cannot
check out the hygiene conditions of the
establishment, a good rule of thumb is if the
bathrooms are spotless, so is the kitchen.

RESTAURANT HOSTING SECRETS

Have you ever considered that restaurant
hosting may wave *three red flags*?
You may not agree with me.
First, you are out of your boardroom comfort
zone. Second, a restaurant environment tends
to reveal more about some people; they drop
their guard, revealing some hidden social
habits, making them more vulnerable.
Third, avoid a restaurant where colleagues
eat out. You may not want to be seen, and
you don't want your conversation interrupted.
If a *friend* does come to your table, be sure
to stand and introduce your guest.

RESTAURANT HOSTING SECRETS

With your invitation, more lead time given increases your guest's importance. Know their dietary needs; ensure they know about parking, restaurant telephone number and dress code.

RESTAURANT HOSTING SECRETS

You have a late guest. If you are seated,
make an effort to stand to shake hands
when your guest does arrive.
Don't show anger; hear the apology with dignity.

RESTAURANT HOSTING SECRETS

You may have eaten at the restaurant before.
And yes, you might make a food a suggestion,
but still let your guest browse the menu.
As for the wine selection, seek the sommelier's
advice; it adds to the theatre of the event.

RESTAURANT HOSTING SECRETS

What? You have a no-show!
What do you do: eat solo or walk away? Here is
where you must display your diplomatic skills. Don't
embarrass your guest when contacting them; hear
their apology with dignity and make another time.

RESTAURANT HOSTING SECRETS

Here is another super business trick:
the secret menu.
If you are a regular diner at this restaurant, go to the
manager, explain the importance of your intended
dining experience. Ask him to print up a special
menu that has, say, two to three entrees, mains, and
desserts, and a variety of wines within your budget.
This menu will not display prices.
On arrival, the waiter will greet you by
name, welcome your entourage, and
walk you to the pre-selected area.
This ruse may cost you a bigger gratuity.

YOU'RE A BUSINESS
DINNER GUEST

THE WHITEBOARD

Here is your dining checklist:

- ✓ Once seated, reverse your table tent card (name tag) if it is printed one-sided, allowing guests to read your name.
- ✓ If given a business card, you can keep it subtly on the dining table for reference. Don't leave other guests' business cards behind when leaving.
- ✓ If your meal is 50/50, i.e. fish/chicken, don't haggle with the waiter. Quietly offer to swap with the person next to you. Don't call attention to your dislike of your meal.
- ✓ Turn your mobile, your Blackberry off, not to vibrate, *to off.* If you are expecting an urgent call, leave it at the receptionist; they will pass you a note.
- ✓ The taking of mobile phone photos in most boardrooms is prohibited mainly due to security.
- ✓ If you drink, remember who's in the room; the most serious of executives only drink water. If the host is insistent, instruct the waiter to pour a quarter of a glass of wine, then leave it.
- ✓ If there is a guest speaker, have your intelligent question ready.
- ✓ If your waiter has a name tag, kindly address them by their name.
- ✓ The serving of coffee/tea is the silent cue that your dining meeting will end in about twenty minutes.

YOU'RE A BUSINESS DINNER GUEST

The further you progress in your career, the more likely you are to both entertain and be entertained. Nowhere are your manners put to the test of scrutiny more than they are at the dining table.

YOU'RE A BUSINESS DINNER GUEST

Your invitation is received.
You're available and you're excited. You
must RSVP, but how? By telephone, email,
SMS, or in person? RSVP is a request for
a response from the host person.
Répondez s'il vous plaît.
The most important thing is to reply. Don't
forget to mention any dietary needs.

YOU'RE A BUSINESS DINNER GUEST

Your arrival

- ✓ Understand the dress culture of both your company and the host company.
- ✓ Don't be early. Don't walk in on the host still placing name tags on the table.
- ✓ If you are running late, you should make every attempt to make contact.
- ✓ When you arrive, apologise once and give a brief explanation.

YOU'RE A BUSINESS DINNER GUEST

The fifteen- to twenty-minute pre-
drink ritual plays two parts:
the opportunity to meet other guests and a
way to allow for late guests. Why should you
not hold your drink in your right hand? Why
should you not carry that pre-meal drinking
glass to the dining table even though you are
halfway through a glass of French bubbles?
This understanding is all part of your exceptional
Etiquette in Business knowledge.

YOU'RE A BUSINESS DINNER GUEST

OK, you have accepted but do not turn up.
What an embarrassing moment. You have been
catered for, a cost to the host that could have
been avoided. There's a gap at the table where
you should be sitting. The other guests have
observed that you're a *no-show*. The company that
you represent must carry this embarrassment.

REQUIRED NETWORKING SKILLS

THE WHITEBOARD

Your pre-networking checklist:

1. Study the registration table/photograph it.
2. Who is hosting/sponsoring this function?
3. Can I contribute at this event?
4. What is the dress code?
5. Name-tag positioning
6. Remember that handshaking is not universal.
7. I must rehearse my elevator speech.
8. Strategies for working the room
9. To drink or not to drink
10. How to begin a conversation
11. How to remember names
12. Can I read their body language?
13. What is the business card protocol?

Having circulated in the room, ask yourself,
'Do I want to be here any longer?'

REQUIRED NETWORKING SKILLS

Networking is the language of connection.
No matter what profession you are in, no
matter what rung on the workplace ladder you
are on, connection is how you succeed.
That's what it's all about.
A successful connection may mean a
change in you. It's that old saying *'It's not
what you know but who you know.'*

REQUIRED NETWORKING SKILLS

Ask yourself, '*Why am I here?*'

✓ To build genuine relationships with people not in my business environment?
✓ To get out of my comfort zone?
✓ To be motivated?

It is not just dropping in for a social
drink on your way home.

It is not just a sly way of promoting
yourself and your business.

REQUIRED NETWORKING SKILLS

Thinking, *I want to network with so-and-so because they can give me an intro to someone I want to do business with* won't work because there is no mutual value. However, if you think, *How can I help this person? Who do I know that might assist their business?* This will work; you're giving something to get something.

REQUIRED NETWORKING SKILLS

What is the dress code?
Casual, semi-formal, or formal? There is no simple answer. Dressing contributes heavily towards creating a positive first impression. Dress for the code of the function. Dress for your personality.

REQUIRED NETWORKING SKILLS

How to make your entrance:

- ✓ Check in the mirror, see how you look.
- ✓ Walk like you're leading your entourage. Never rush into a room. Walk in slowly, smile, and pause for a few minutes before entering the room.
- ✓ Don't act as an unofficial greeter by stationing yourself near the door, ensuring that you don't miss *important guests*.

REQUIRED NETWORKING SKILLS

The world is based on reality vs. perception.
People's perception of you is your secret.
Focus on meeting only a handful of people; the
key to your success is access to this opportunity.
Be interested. Be enthusiastic.
Avoid interrupting in mid-sentence.
Don't criticise anyone or anything.

REQUIRED NETWORKING SKILLS

Understand that networking is about building
relationships, not just promoting your own.
Every business has people from different
cultures, generations, and knowledge skills.
Excite people when they want to know about you.

REQUIRED NETWORKING SKILLS

Having a flaw in your DNA should not affect
your intelligence or ability to network.
While in your mind you may think that you are
not the smartest person in the room, *stop*!
The evidence will show that if you have the
ability to connect and relate to others, you
have just shown that you are an equal.

REQUIRED NETWORKING SKILLS

Meeting with people, talking to people is your glue.
Your success can be based on the opportunity to
connect with people from different walks of life.
Everyone you will ever meet knows
something that you don't. This collective
wisdom will help you go forward.

REQUIRED NETWORKING SKILLS

Our cultural background influences our
communication styles, e.g. how close
we stand to a person (personal space),
eye contact, and forms of address.

REQUIRED NETWORKING SKILLS

The best moment to hand a business card
is when you're asked for one, *or* when
you're asked to repeat your name, *or* when
someone offers to send you something.
When handing your card, you may say,
'I think I can help you with . . .'

REQUIRED NETWORKING SKILLS

To start your conversation, bring out your *big guns*,
your most powerful tools: your smile, appropriate
eye contact, and that proper handshake.
Three topics to start a conversation:
(1) The situation. (2) The other person. (3) You.
Three ways to begin a conversation:
(1) Ask a question. (2) Give an opinion.
(3) State a fact.

REQUIRED NETWORKING SKILLS

Practice being last to speak.
Listen carefully as other networkers introduce
themselves and how they explain what they
do and what they are looking to accomplish
while they are there. Being last to speak is an
art that has to be learnt and cultivated.
Negotiate like a pro. Build your
brand. Leave a legacy.

REQUIRED NETWORKING SKILLS

Remembering names is an art.
The truth is most people have trouble remembering
names; this is because our memories are not
designed to learn names through verbal cues.
Our memory works through image, action,
and emotion. It might be a perfume,
accent, their height. Silently turn their
name into a picture; it might be fun.
It might drive you around the
bend, but try it anyway.

REQUIRED NETWORKING SKILLS

Whether you are the CEO or the office junior, you are on an equal playing field when networking. Display your communication skills, your social skills, your body language, and your confidence.

REQUIRED NETWORKING SKILLS

You can gain confidence by talking into a mirror.
Know what your facial expressions look like,
both right and left, albeit they are in reverse.
Try it; it works.
Practice your introduction in front of this
mirror; note what you need to improve.
Regardless of your career status, it's your
branding that makes you visible.

REQUIRED NETWORKING SKILLS

Don't limit yourself to business networking.
When we think of networking, we should
think of business events, functions, cultural
associations, even volunteering.

REQUIRED NETWORKING SKILLS

We all need escape lines.

'Great to meet with you, Jack, thanks for the conversation.'

'Wow. I've learned a lot from this conversation, Mary. I know we're both here to network, so why don't we?'

'I'd like to chat with you more about this. Do you have a business card?'

The important thing here is to say something, as long as it is polite.

BUSINESS CARD PROTOCOL

THE WHITEBOARD

- ✓ Buy a card holder.
- ✓ Carry blank cards.
- ✓ Don't scribble notes on the back, except in private.
- ✓ Don't fan your cards out; it's not a poker game. Offer one only.
- ✓ Don't stack cards for people to help themselves; you must know the receiver.
- ✓ Present your card face up; never toss it across the table.
- ✓ Show interest when receiving and reading a business card; know the cultural custom of the giver and how to pronounce their name.
- ✓ If your card is bilingual, have it translated professionally.
- ✓ Be discerning when offering your card. Use your judgement, don't give your card to someone you know you will not connect with.

BUSINESS CARD PROTOCOL

Business cards are something that we take for granted when we shouldn't. The look, feel, and message on a card help people determine how they view you and, more importantly, if they will even remember you.

BUSINESS CARD PROTOCOL

Your card represents the current sum of your efforts. Respect yours and others'. Your business card is your greatest means of introduction to the world, the best source of business correspondence.

BUSINESS CARD PROTOCOL

Networking is not complete without receiving or giving a business card. Always make a comment about a card when you receive it. Note the logo, the business name, or some other piece of information. You have no card? Carry blanks.

BUSINESS CARD PROTOCOL

In large meetings/lunches/dinners where, say, multiple persons are from the same company, keep all cards in front of you to remind you of their pecking order.

BUSINESS CARD PROTOCOL

The world has its own unwritten code.
Some business cards have little meaning other
than essential personal details, while others
are treated as an extension of the person.

HEARING IS NOT LISTENING

THE WHITEBOARD

Common barriers to listening

✓ Listening to more than one conversation at a time
✓ Distracted by the speaker's looks, good or bad
✓ You have no interest in the conversation.
✓ You are distracted by noise or bad lighting.
✓ You are biased.
✓ The speaker has a strong accent.
✓ The speaker has no eye contact with you.

HEARING IS NOT LISTENING

A wise old owl lived in an oak
The more he saw, the less he spoke
The less he spoke, the more he heard
Why can't we all be like that wise old bird?

HEARING IS NOT LISTENING

Did you realise that listening and hearing are not the same? One way to become a better listener is to familiarise yourself with the major distinctions between listening and hearing. You cannot be a good leader unless you are a good listener.

HEARING IS NOT LISTENING

Hearing is a natural process.
To hear, all you have to do is be there. Listening
is a learned process; this involves focusing on the
speaker and what is being said, processing what is
being said, and remembering what is being said.

HEARING IS NOT LISTENING

Listening gives everybody the feeling
that they have been heard. It lets people
feel that they have contributed.
By listening, you will understand what they mean
and why they have the opinion that they have.

HEARING IS NOT LISTENING

The ability to listen carefully will allow you to have a
better understanding of what is expected of you.
When you genuinely show interest, you
strengthen your connection with that person.

HEARING IS NOT LISTENING

Did you realise that when you are talking, you are only repeating something that you already know, but if you listen, you may learn something new. Remembering a name or a special detail from a conversation could give you that competitive edge.

MENTORS: PURPOSE
AND VALUE

MENTORS: PURPOSE AND VALUE

In my career, I had several mentors who believed in, supported, encouraged, and cheered me on to maximise my potential, developing my skills to improve my attitude, allowing me to become the person I am today. Each mentor gave me a different perspective, challenging me to do my own thinking I did my best. I'm glad I'm me.

MENTORS: PURPOSE AND VALUE

In order for you to be a top sportsperson,
wouldn't you have a coach?
It is the same in business.
We all don't begin from the same starting point.
We all need coaching, and like the athlete, the
manner in which we perform dictates our progress.

MENTORS: PURPOSE AND VALUE

How do you find this coach, this mentor?
Your starting line involves not only finding a
mentor, but also finding *the right mentor*.
The idea is not simply to find someone
successful, well-educated, and willing to mentor
you. It goes far beyond convenience. The
mentor you chose (and who chose you) should
be someone who is equipped to mentor in
your field and who's in it for the long run.
Ideally, it is also someone who shares, at least to
some extent, your morals, integrity, and ambition.

MENTORS: PURPOSE AND VALUE

Learn from their failures and their ability
to acknowledge those failures.
Learn from their mistakes.
Use these lessons and apply these to your daily life.

MENTORS: PURPOSE AND VALUE

Follow your mentors' lead; they will
encourage you to remove your blinkers
and enable you to add value.
Never pretend to know all the answers.
Surround yourself with progressive people.
When they say,
'Can you do it?' you say, 'Watch me.'

MENTORS: PURPOSE AND VALUE

Let your mentor see what is in your backpack.
It will help them set you clear and objective
goals, the most fundamental tasks in
building your career, enabling you to add
value to both yourself and others.
Listen to them. Distil their wisdom.
Apply it to your journey.

MENTORS: PURPOSE AND VALUE

When life throws you a challenge, don't
try to be better than anyone else, just
be better than you used to be.
Mentors will teach you business protocol
and show you how to be a better person.
Be smart enough to listen.

MENTORS: PURPOSE AND VALUE

Outstanding people do not emerge from a formula.
If you do things like everybody else,
you will be like everybody else.
Mentors will encourage you to
do things that others don't do, see
things that others don't see, take risks,
and create your point of difference.

MENTORS: PURPOSE AND VALUE

In simple terms, mentors give you a hand up.
In this *win-win* situation, the rewards are
many, the risks are non-existent; listen to
them, watch them, not because of what they
do but who they are and how they do it.
Do the homework that they give you,
and then embrace their knowledge.

MENTORS: PURPOSE AND VALUE

Mentoring is guiding and advising you
in your personal development to reach
your highest potential based on their
personal and professional experiences.
They could be either paid or non-paid.

MENTORS: PURPOSE AND VALUE

Develop a relationship with someone you
admire personally, not because of what they
do but who they are and how they do it.
They don't even have to be in your workplace.
This mentor will help you find yourself,
encourage you to remove your blinkers.
You will be asking questions you
never thought to ask.

OK, you're at the end of my
Pocket Inspirations on Etiquette in Business.
Keep this book handy; it will help you with
your personal goals. Have fun at your job.

THE
BUSINESS ETIQUETTE
CONSULTANCY

PO Box 88
East Melbourne, Victoria 8002
Email: info@businessetiquette.com.au
Web: www.businessetiquette.com.au
Mobile: (0412) 554 353

THE
BUSINESS ETIQUETTE
CONSULTANCY

Lightning Source UK Ltd.
Milton Keynes UK
UKHW012102270220
359474UK00001B/38/J

9 781984 505293